THEATRE IN CORPORATE

RAJEEV RANJAN

Made with ♥ on the Notion Press Platform
www.notionpress.com

To

Renu Devi & Surendra Rai

Contents

PREFACE

Here it is, the theatre-meets-corporate-training welcome you to a learning experience of the cutting edge. In this book, "Theatre in Corporate" we are going to discuss the connection between the two fields and the potential to transform the practice when it comes to the employees' development.

The basis for this book was attempted for several years of observation and testing of the shift on the effects of theatrical methods in different types of corporations. At the same time, for me all my experiences proved that theatre is an engaging and effective strategy for training different skills that cannot be developed with the use of simple non-applicable methods.

Today's business environment expresses efficiency measurements, financial performance, and tangible outcomes, however, top-performing companies understand the importance of an enthusiastic, dedicated, and creative staff. Theatre, which locates its focus on a narration, mimicry, and scenario, can be considered as the kind of training that will enhance these features significantly. It enables people to step into the shoes of other people, and they are exposed to practising various interpersonal skills that are very useful in the current world economy.

In this book, the reader will discover numerous examples of the practical application of exercises, case descriptions, and theoretical concepts that are helpful in the process of implementing the notions from the theatre into corporate training. All of the chapters are designed to offer a clear understanding of different topics concerning the flow of processes and relations, including leading people, teaming, maintaining stress, and increasing well-being.

The first chapter finds the psychological bases of learning through theatre performance. Considering other theories in the field of psychology, this chapter proves the applicability and efficiency of the theatre activities used in corporations. Topics such as Social Learning Theory, Experiential Learning Theory, and

Cognitive Load Theory that indicate how social learning is used in various organisations to enhance communication, leadership, Interpersonal communication and teamwork in business organisations.

Chapter two is thus dedicated to the introduction to the use of theatre in training within business organisations to lay the groundwork for the subsequent chapters. The following points will be covered, such as the use of storytelling and its potential in enhancing the outcomes of communication in the company.

Chapter three revolves around role playing and simulation pointing out practical guidelines on how to develop and use effective scenarios that foster problem solving, conflict solving, and sensitization. Such activities are not only entertaining but also serve as excellent training tables for the participants to be content with working on their skills.

One of the essential aspects of any business organisation is communication, and from chapter four, one learns that skills such as modulating the voice, involving the use of the body while speaking and even listening keenly will go a long way in improving communication in corporate organisations. Several of the techniques described in the book are best applied through hands-on exercises, and corresponding workshops, which can be integrated into the training programs.

Chapter five therefore focuses on the methods of the leadership competencies and the importance of incorporating theatre in order to promote teamwork values. Trust building activities such as trust walks, construction of charades, and the inclusion of a series of role plays are provided with clear and understandable instructions that should help leaders or trainers to make their teams better.

Chapter six focuses on the creativity and innovation that is brought about by the theatre. You will learn about the connection between the creative exercises such as improvisation and the enhancement of creative and problem-solving abilities at the workplace within your organisation. Examples from the field are used to show how these techniques are implemented in today's organisations.

Health and welfare are vital in any organisation, and chapter seven shows exactly how theatre can be used in encouraging people in the workplace to express themselves, relaxed and happy. Examples of the areas include drama as a therapy, use of images, breathing exercises as well as workshop sessions aimed at promoting employees' health.

Chapter eight relates to diversity and inclusion; we illustrate how theatre can be effective in eliminating prejudice, increasing understanding, and improving workplace diversity. The focus is given to the descriptions of role-play scenarios, perspective-taking activities, and diversity conversations that contain the recommendations on how to improve the organisational climate for diversity.

Chapter nine of the book provides the reader with an insightful and informative manual on how to put into practice theatre based programs in corporate organisations. In this chapter, you are shown how to successfully implement theatre methods in your training endeavours starting right from determining goals and how to design the program, prepare training tools and resources, training of the facilitators and finally, how to assess the effects of this approach.

Chapter ten focuses on the various and complex tasks of the corporate theatre trainer. The following chapter is designed to explain why this position entails demand for both theatrical orientation and business savvy. Topics highlighted include role of trainer including needs analysis, course development and delivery, feedback and determination of programme outcomes. Furthermore, the chapter outlines such effective qualities as interpersonal skills, compassion, report aged and moderate flexibility that are vital in the process of endeavouring to unite theatre and business training. Useful tips and examples are included so that a trainer is able to apply tips given to design memorable, changer-making training.

The path you are about to follow will be creative, involved, and transformative. What is revealed here is that by willingly embracing the principles of theatre there is always a room for growth and success in relation to the organisational structures. This book is more than a compilation of ideas and practicalities: it is a call to decouple effective business education from what is normal and therefore discover the wealth of theatre holds for corporations.

I hope you enjoyed this adventure as much as I did and thank you for being with me. It is my wish that this book will be of help to you in ensuring that theatrics is incorporated in corporate training thereby making workplaces more lively, creative and supportive. Let the journey begin!

So, it is possible to reveal the previously unseen potential of training and the areas of applicability for theatre techniques in the sphere of enterprise learning. This book will be your initiator into the understanding of how the principles of the theatre apply to professional development. Regardless if you are a new trainer or an experienced one, I wish that you can take something from this book and apply it in your practice to be able to leave a positive impact in the world.

Happy reading and best of luck to your corporate escapades steeped in the justification of theatre.

Introduction

On the surface the theatre industry and business world seem to be miles apart. But they have some fundamental principles in common – both are driven by great performances, strong storytelling and effective communication. Theatre techniques are being used by businesses to engage employees, develop leaders and stimulate creativity. This book looks at how corporations can tap into the power of theatre.

Brief History of Theatre in Corporate Training

In the long history of theatre itself, corporate training is a relatively new development but the roots can be traced back to ancient practices where performance was used as a teaching and social reflection tool.

Early Foundations:

Drama was a key part of civic education in ancient Greece where the practice of using theatre for education began. Philosophers like Aristotle used theatre to study human behaviour, ethics and social norms, recognising its therapeutic and educational value. Morality plays which used allegorical characters and stories to teach audiences about virtues and vices continued theatre's didactic role into the mediaeval era.

Modern Applications:

Mid 20th century the modern practice of using theatre in corporate training started to take shape. Companies were looking for new ways to improve employee communication, leadership and teamwork. This was in response to the need for more sophisticated organisational practices as industrialisation took hold. Theatre which focuses on empathy, expression and teamwork emerged as a tool for these goals.

Theatre in business has often been traced back to Augusto Boal's Theatre of the Oppressed which is one of the earliest well-known implementations of theatrical performance in the commercial world. His methods (role-playing and workshops) were originally created for political and social problems solving. But corporate training was in line with empowerment, active participation and reflection made the employees to improve on understanding organisational politics and how to handle conflicts.

Growth and Formalisation:

Theatre-based corporate training expanded and formalised in the 80s and 90s. Businesses started to hire professional actors and theatre practitioners to create bespoke programs as they recognised the value of experiential learning. Soft skills like leadership, emotional intelligence and communication were the focus of these programs. Simulation games, role-playing and improvisation are now common in corporate training modules. The growing field of applied theatre legitimised the use of theatrical techniques in non-traditional settings like the workplace. Frameworks and methods for integrating organisational development with theatre arts were developed by academics and practitioners.

Modern Practices:

Theatre in corporate training is now a mainstream practice used by companies worldwide. To create immersive and impactful learning experiences, modern programs often combine the latest technologies like virtual reality and digital simulations with traditional theatre techniques. Intercultural theatre practices which help employees navigate and celebrate cultural differences have also been brought into the workplace with the rise of global and diverse workplaces. And the focus has moved from just addressing competencies and skills to a more holistic approach to employee development. Creativity, mental health, teams that are adaptable and resilient are all examples of this. Because it makes people step out of their comfort zones, actively solve problems and build strong relationships, theatre based training has been shown to be especially effective in these areas.

How businesses can use theatrical techniques

The Power of Storytelling

Storytelling is powerful in business and theatre. Stories engage audiences, evoke emotions and convey deep meaning in theatre. Similarly a company's vision, values and objectives can be told through storytelling in business. When it comes to motivating and inspiring their team's leaders who can craft and tell a good story do better.

Communication and Presentation Skills

Operational and theatrical success is based on good communication. To make sure their messages are heard and have an impact actors go through intense training to learn how to communicate verbally and non verbally. These skills can help you make presentations, negotiate and interact with people better in the workplace. The techniques from theatre that can help corporate professionals become more persuasive and engaging communicators will be covered in this book.

Team Dynamics and Collaboration

In every performance, the team has to comprise directors, actors and designers and technicians among others and the synergy of all these members is very critical in enhancing the production. People of different ranks work towards the achievement of a successful show. As such, a similar level of cooperation in the work setting can result in better solutions and a united team. We will consider how exactly drama improvisations and exercises can be applied to the problems of teamwork and cooperation at work.

Leadership and Presence

Assertiveness is one more important aspect, which is inherent in every good director and actor on the stage. Hence in business leadership it is of equal importance. Building your persona, the means and the values will assist you to manage effectively and communicate with your people more effectively.

Creativity and Innovation

This is because; theatre is an aspect of drama which is viewed as art and creativity that keeps on testing the conventional and developing new concepts. In an environment where competitiveness breeds in business, this creative mindset is worth a fortune. Using theatrical techniques, it is possible to make companies instil appropriate values and make their workers start thinking beyond the horizon.

Coping with change and alteration

On stage actors need to be versatile and be able to alter directions at short notice. The fact that business in today's scenario is less about stableness and more about dynamism, the concept of flexibility becomes imperative. By engaging in theoretical exercises corporate workers may be trained to become stronger in order to withstand the modernising business environment.

Conclusion

Some ideas and thoughts could be opened for the corporate training and development process if theatre concepts are introduced to business. Read in this book to find out how you can positively change your corporate world. If you are a leader, who wants to motivate your workers, a business person, who needs such skills or an organisation whose goals are to promote effective teamwork and introduce an innovative approach, this book will be useful.

I

The Psychology Behind Theatre-Based Learning

Psychological concepts that support theatre based learning.

The advantage of Theatre-Based Learning can be traced in psychological theories that indicate how people learn, communicate and acquire skills. A comprehension of these theories is beneficial for the creation of perspective and substantiation of effective theatre-based training interventions. Thus, in this chapter chosen psychological theories will be described along with examples of their application in corporate theatre-based learning.

1. Social Learning Theory

Social Learning Theory by Albert Bandura, the major postulate leans on the observation, legitimate modelling and reproduction of the behaviour, affective and cognitive responses of other people.

Bandura's theory highlights four key processes in social learning: learning involves paying attention, getting ideas retained in a memorable manner, reproduction and motivation are regarded as the fundamental aspects of learning.

Application in Theatre-Based Learning:

Observation and Modeling: participators see how good communication and leadership practices are implemented through the trainers or peers while imitating what they have been taught in role-play roles.

Retention: By the end of the demonstration the participants have the opportunity to keep on observing the different behaviours and assimilate all the skills being taught.

Reproduction: In one's actual working environment, the participants are encouraged to perform what they have learned, thus increasing the efficiency of the particular skills in the real world.

Motivation: The motivation of the learners is therefore boosted through positive reinforcements which are associated with theatre exercises.

Example: It is quite possible that during the role-playing, the subject will witness how a facilitator properly resolves a conflict. They then apply the aforesaid techniques, get corrected, and are encouraged to use the skills in their working setting.

2. Experiential Learning Theory

Experiential Learning Theory has been developed by David Kolb that believes and states that learning is a process that occurs when information is transformed into knowledge. Kolb's learning cycle consists of four stages: grounded understanding, observation, thinking about the experience, and finally active mode of experiencing.

Application in Theatre-Based Learning:

Concrete Experience: There are theatre activities performed which include role play, improvisation and storytelling, this gives the participants actual experience.

Reflective Observation: Follow-up questions are encouraged to occur after the activities where the participants are allowed to discuss what happened, how they felt and what they saw.

Abstract Conceptualization: Participants make conclusions or generalise from the things they consider; they comprehend the principles on which they work.

Active Experimentation: They use new knowledge in different aspects and settings, hence, consciously or unconsciously, try what does not work and what flows smoothly.

Example: A person who passes through a leadership workshop traumatises him or her in some ways though in this case the person has to guide a team through a project. On completion , it turns into contemplating on how they performed it, sharing the gains with other workers, expounding the leadership principles, and putting into practice the leadership principles in their working stations.

3. Cognitive Load Theory

Working memory capacity is defined by Cognitive Load Theory created by John Sweller, which concerns the quantity of information that can be processed simultaneously. It defines cognitive load into intrinsic, extraneous, and germane and stresses on the importance of the appropriate regulation of the cognitive load.

Application in Theatre-Based Learning:

Intrinsic Load: There are always theatre activities meant to correspond to the levels at which content is delivered, so as not to handicap the learner with the level of difficulty or boredom him or her with the amount of ease.

Extraneous Load: As for the Amsterdam tradition theatre exercises, one has to reduce additional cognitive load by simplifying the instructions and eliminating possible distractions.

Germane Load: Effective implementation of meaningful activities helps learners to be more engaged with the learning material thus making it easier for them to understand and remember the content fed to them.

Example: During the communication skills session, clients are taken through basic mechanical drills hence they begin with such structures. The tasks also gradually increase in difficulty; however, the instructions are well-defined and pertinent to prevent overwhelming the participants' working memory capacity.

4. Emotional Contagion Theory

Emotional Contagion Theory posits that clients may receive feelings from other people via formal and informal interactions. This theory emphasises the belonging of people to distinct groups and their emotional interaction as a way of influencing the learning process.

Application in Theatre-Based Learning:

Positive Emotions: Amiable feelings like joy, excitement, pleasure, and satisfaction increases the engagement level and motivation of the learners as per the theatre activities.

Shared Experiences: Group exercises produce team feelings, and mutual, shared strain, which helps in establishing an atmosphere of learning support.

Feedback and Reflection: The facilitators ensure that they comment positively and also support any constructive criticism that may be given by other participants to be given in a positive manner.

Example: In the course of a group improvisation, the favourable attitude of participants due to their liking enhances everyone's desire to perform and come up with more great ideas. Group construction helps build team cohesion since a number of organisations apply or encourage the creation of a story or fable as part of a lesson.

5. Transformational Leadership Theory

The Transformational Leadership Theory was propounded by James MacGregor Burns and was later developed by Bernard Bass and this kind of leadership entails the casting of a new and superior light into followers, thus making them transform into better performers. It is also termed as the VIF theory and it largely focuses on vision, inspiration, and intellectual stimulation that leaders bring about.

Application in Theatre-Based Learning:

Vision and Inspiration: Some include preparing the participants to describe a persuasive vision and be able to coax the group into following them.

Intellectual Stimulation: Theatre problem solving or activities that involve individuals to think and come up with the most productive solution.

Individualised Consideration: Leadership coaching tends to form the core of the facilitators' activity in order to help people uncover strengths within.

Example: In a leadership development workshop activity, whereby the participants have to manage a team, through a business-like scenario. They train on how to motivate a team, promote creativity, and empower people in the subordinate groups.

6. Theory of Multiple Intelligences

Thus Howard's Multiple Intelligences indicate that a person has some different abilities including the verbal, logical, spatial and mathematical, musical, physical and mover, interpersonal and intrapersonal and ecological.

Application in Theatre-Based Learning:

Linguistic Intelligence: Technique and devising games that focus on the improvement of spoken and written language.

Bodily-Kinesthetic Intelligence: Skills of dramatic movements such as gestures and body movements which are a type of the physical theatre.

Interpersonal Intelligence: Such activities as pair or group assignments that address feelings, recognition, and relationship with others.

Intrapersonal Intelligence: Some seminars involve activities, which are designed to make individuals be more aware of themselves and the world around them.

Example: A theatre-based learning program comprises of dramatic play and writing, which involves an enactment of a play and narration– linguistic and bodily-kinesthetic intelligence, group drama, which involves creating a play with others–interpersonal intelligence, and individual reflection on the performance, which involves assessing one's own performance–intrapersonal intelligence.

7. Positive Psychology

Positive Psychology was pioneered by Martin Seligman and Mihaly Csikszent; Positive psychology deals with the study of positive experience, traits and the components, which contribute to optimum living.

Application in Theatre-Based Learning:

Strengths-Based Approach: Theatre activities that focus on the participants' assets and the ways of applying them in different situations.

Positive Emotions: Aerobic activities that elicit pleasurable emotions and increase the disposition towards happiness including contentment, positivity, and hope.

Flow State: Coster stepped up tasks that are not too demanding but at the same time not too easy so that persons are optimally involved in what they are doing hence gaining the state of flow.

Example: Possibly in a team-building workshop people are encouraged to act out small stories which are true and encompass victories as well as assets. This does not only increase individual morale but also has the same effect on the morale of a team.

8. Broaden-and-Build Theory

The Broaden-and-Build Theory which Fredrickson proposed indicates that positive emotions expand the range of thoughts and behaviours that people can imagine and implement in addition to strengthening one's bodily, cognitive, and social capital.

Application in Theatre-Based Learning:

Broadened Perspective: Theatre exercises which will help to focus on creative thinking and shift to new opportunities.

Building Resources: Such activities that may relate mainly to social, learning and motor skills.

Example: There is an activity that takes the form of a group improvisation where the objectives are for participants to be creative and work together. They are happy and therefore develop a wider perspective towards the subject that enhances and cements their relation within the team.

Conclusion

A deeper appreciation of theories of psychology applied in the use of theatre based learning creates a good foundation in the formulation of training strategies that help in the development of good learning programs. Utilising principles from social learning, experiential learning, cognitive overload theory, emotional contagion, transformational leadership, multiple intelligence, positive psychology, and broadening and building theory, it is possible to design theatre-based learning as the type of learning that can build up the self and profession. Therefore, as trainers and facilitators keep on developing and implementing the above mentioned theories, Theatre for Learning will remain a profound approach to Personal, Psychological, Creative and Organisational Development in corporations.

II

The Power of Storytelling

Business Storytelling

Effective storytelling techniques used in the social field and modern technologies are the necessary tools for addressing the target audience, conveying certain messages, or mobilising actions in business. In the manner of theatre, the presentation is delicate; the power to narrate a good story is eloquent between a message that is taken to heart or one that is dismissed. It is worth to note that they explain such or such, put into context or humanise information.

Humanising Data

Data is the king in the business world. Thus, to make rational decisions, such concepts as metrics, statistics, and numbers are crucial. However, data by itself is quite sterile and unemotional. Through storytelling, data is made less intimidating and is made in a way that would be easy to understand and even in a way one would find interesting. For instance, qualitative data like sales figures transformed into the story of how customers are satisfied and the business's growth are likely to be more persuasive than just raw numbers.

Context

Thus, I would like to emphasise that without context information might be rather misleading and even intimidating. Reference is given by narrative which helps to categorise data into comprehensible patterns that have been found efficient to encode. Information presentation should follow chronological order that changes with human's development and experience that are seen in good stories. Thus, the audience not only grasps the information but receives it in this manner.

Making Abstract Concepts Relatable

Vision, mission and values are some of the more abstract concepts businesses deal with. It can be hard to communicate these. Storytelling makes these concepts relatable by using examples and scenarios from real life. Leaders can help stakeholders and employees understand and accept these abstract concepts by telling stories that embody the company's values or mission.

Theatre Techniques

Theatre has many storytelling techniques that can be applied directly to business. Here are a few:

Building a Narrative Arc

A good narrative arc keeps the reader engaged and takes them on a journey. In business this means making a presentation or pitch that has a clear beginning, middle and end so the main point gets across. The setup of the main idea and setting the scene is in the beginning, the development of the narrative with supporting details and examples in the middle and the big message or call to action at the end.

Using Emotion to Connect

Emotion connects people. It teaches concepts about the utilisation of emotion in storytelling in the aspect of theatre. This means comprehending which feelings are attached to the words that you are going to use in order to establish a more profound business rapport. It is always more effective to follow the rules of an agenda and call on feelings like the feeling of a new product release on the market or the feeling of having a problem that needs to be solved urgently or the feeling of inspiration looking at the success story .

Character Development

Stories are driven by people. These can be customers, employees or even the brand itself in business storytelling. The story becomes more interesting and relatable when these characters are given personality and depth. A human element is added to the story by highlighting a customer's journey or an employee's achievements.

Setting

The environment and context is provided by the setting. Whether it's a busy startup office or a calm multinational corporation's headquarters, describing the setting helps the audience see the scene. This theatrical technique makes business presentations more immersive and memorable.

Conflict and Resolution

Every good story has tension and a happy ending. This could be a company's problems and how they overcame them in business. This adds drama and keeps the audience interested. And it shows resilience and problem solving skills which are highly valued in business.

Case Studies

Look at these examples to see how storytelling works in business:

Apple

Apple's product launches are quite memorable in the way they tell stories. Rather than merely stating dimensions of the product, each presentation is a story. For instance, when the iPhone first emerged, instead of enumerating the benefits of the device, Steve Jobs said. He recanted a story about mobile technology and evolution and how the iPhone came to be and was basically a tool that revolutionised how people communicate with each other and the world.

TED Talks

What I soon came to realise is that TED speakers are fantastic storytellers. They express them using stories from their own lives, raise appeal to emotion, and tell stories that attract listeners. TED talk is not a lecture as well as performance with elements of theatre and personas who tell the truth in the most easy-to-understand and funny way. For instance, the talk done by Brené Brown where she shares the story of vulnerability and supports this with research to enable millions of people to relate to the situation.

Nike

Nike advertising campaigns are styled to sell Nike's products but at the same time, they are narrating stories. For instance, the 'Just Do It' campaign, takes inspiring stories of athletes who conquer, are inspired and turn into great athletes. Nike becomes a believable force of inspiration, of coming through for the athletes, for the struggling ones, for the ones who have never given up in one way or the other and these are the audiences; The audience is touched by these stories which also reminds them of Nike's relating core values of Perseverance, inspiration, performance.

Dove

An example of business storytelling could be the "Real Beauty' campaign for Dove. Dove shared stories that were contrary to what was normally expected as the definition of beauty and boosted the morale of women without promoting their soaps. This made the story interesting to its target public and at the same time, made Dove a company with a conscience of the health of its consumers.

Airbnb

These are not new concepts, what Airbnb has done well, and which has largely contributed to its success, is its storytelling. Airbnb is also involved in sharing the experiences of both the hosts and guests and develops a social contract. The brand becomes more human and more reliable because of these stories which show one off travel experiences and personal connections made through the platform.

Telling Your Business Story

What's Your Message?

What shall be the moral lesson of your story before you write the content of the story for the people to understand? So what do you want them to remember a week later, a month later? Their recommendations are generally short, clear and focused on your business objectives.

Who's Your Audience?

Preferably, discover who your target market is. Their wants, needs, and major concerns are as follows: It is thus better told, if it is first customised to their needs.

The next assignment entails coming up with a story, which has to have cohesive elements such as; intensity, climax, and denouement. Start conflicts in the beginning part, introduce the characters, the environment and the conflict. A news report should be brought out with examples and the supporting information and the report should end with a conclusion together with a call for action.

Add Emotion

In this case one should not be afraid to express emotions. These are feelings such as joy, fear, excitement or inspiration ; they help to add an attraction to stories.

Practice and Refine

Like other skills, storytelling improves with experience thus the frequent telling of the story. Do the best you can on your story, and try it out, discuss it and make the best version of it.

Conclusion

The art of telling a story is dead-on when it comes to business. Thus, it becomes possible for businesses to project engaging, informative, and inspiring stories by employing elements of theatre. Irrespective of the reason, which is to serve your audience with a presentation, introduce a new product, or share the core values of your organisation, storytelling allows for attaining your business objectives and building a stronger bond with your audience. More examples and practical use will be given as before as we progress.

III

Role-Playing and Simulation

What is Role-Playing

Things like simulation and play acting where persons and behaviours are adopted for a particular behaviour or series of behaviours to be tested. It is applied in the theatre to grow personalities as well as in corporate training to depict real life situations. In theatre, the actors implement the concept of 'getting into the skin of the character,' to comprehend the character's feelings and behaviours. To be more concrete, in the corporate world, employees apply role playing to enter into different roles, to look at events or phenomena from different angles, and to test out different strategies of solving problems and communicating.

How to Design Role-Plays

Creating realistic and relevant scenarios is key to effective role-playing. Here are the steps:

Setting Clear Objectives

Before you start a role-play you need to decide what you want to achieve. Objectives can be anything from improving customer service skills and conflict resolution strategies to team working and leadership skills. Clear objectives mean the role-play is focused and participants know what the exercise is about.

Crafting Realistic Scenarios

The effectiveness of a role-play depends on the scenarios. Scenarios should reflect real life challenges employees will face in their roles. This could be dealing with a difficult customer, managing a team under time pressure or navigating a complex negotiation. The more realistic the scenario the better the role-play will be. It helps participants fully engage and apply what they are learning in a practical way.

Role Assignment

Role assignment is key. Participants should be given roles that stretch them but also play to their strengths. Role assignment can also be an opportunity to build empathy by having participants play roles they don't normally play, e.g. a manager as a frontline employee or vice versa.

Implementation

Here's how to do role-plays in the workplace:

Briefing

Start with a briefing where you explain what the role-play is about and what the objectives are. Give background and context so participants know the scenario and their role. Clarity here means success in the role-play.

Action

Perform the part of the role-play, let participants act out the case. Be loose and let it flow as much as possible. What is then needed is an environment that will allow participants to risk and fail if they so wish. This is where the learning happens.

Debrief

Ensuring everyone is back to their normal and usual self, wrap up the episodes by doing a debrief. Debrief the event, what happened, what was effective and what was not. Of course, discuss the results of the learning process and how they can be used in everyday life. Post debriefing is important, they further reinforce the learning and give feedback and an opportunity to reflect.

Case Studies

Role-playing has been used by many companies to improve skills and performance. Here are a few examples:

Deloitte

Deloitte uses role-playing in their leadership training to help managers develop better communication and conflict resolution skills. In these sessions managers are put in difficult scenarios where they have to navigate conflicts, give feedback and motivate their teams. Through role-playing they practise and sharpen their leadership skills in a safe environment so they are ready for real life.

American Express

American Express uses role-playing exercises in their customer service training to prepare employees for dealing with difficult customer interactions. Employees act out scenarios with angry customers, complex service issues and high pressure situations. These exercises help them develop the skills to stay calm, empathetic and effective under pressure.

Google

Specific examples of the interventions being used are Google diversity and inclusion system that employs role play. Special attention is paid to the tasks based on the conflicts arising from the prejudices, cultural differences, and leadership styles. The role play enables the participants to realise their prejudice and which assists in making the workplace environment to be more acceptable.

Procter & Gamble

Role-playing is employed in the Marketing training by Procter & Gamble. Employees adopt the customer, competitor as well as the partner perspectives to simulate different roles in improving promotional strategies.

Marriott International

Marriott International uses role-playing in their hospitality training. Employees simulate guest interactions from check-in to dealing with complaints to ensure they deliver exceptional service. These exercises help staff develop the skills and confidence to improve the guest experience.

Role-Playing Tips

To get the most out of role-playing in corporate training:

Create a Safe Space

Make sure the role-playing is in a safe and non-threatening environment. Participants should feel free to try and make mistakes.

Get Everyone Involved

Get all participants fully into their roles. The more they are in character the more they will learn from the experience.

Give Feedback

In the debrief, get constructive feedback that focuses on strengths and areas for improvement. Ask participants to reflect on their own performance and what they took away.

Swap Roles

Consider swapping roles in subsequent role-playing sessions. This allows participants to see things from different perspectives and develop more skills.

Use Different Scenarios

Use a variety of scenarios to cover different areas of the business and different challenges employees may face. This keeps the training interesting and relevant.

Conclusion

It is clear that role-play and simulation are fruitful in the corporate training, which is an effective means of creating a similar functioning environment and mastering actual work experience. Hereby presenting how theatre techniques can assist businesses in designing effective and interesting role play activities within the focused skills of communication, leadership, and solving problems. As we continue to explore the intersection of theatre and business we will discover more ways to develop employees and organisations.

IV
Communication Skills

Core Theatre Techniques

Theatre techniques provide a great foundation for developing communication skills. By focusing on voice, body and active listening individuals can communicate more clearly and connect with others.

1. Voice

Pitch Control

Pitch control is key to emphasis and keeping the audience engaged. Exercises can help you practise varying your pitch:

Monotone vs Varied Pitch: Have the participants read a passage in a monotone voice, then re-read it with varied pitch to highlight the key points. This exercise shows how pitch variation affects the listener.

Pitch Range Exercises: Have the participants practise their vocal range by doing scales and varying pitch within sentences. This helps them feel more comfortable using different pitches naturally.

Tone and Emotion

Tone conveys emotion and intention. Practising tone variation helps you express different emotions:

Emotional Phrases: Have the participants practise saying the phrase "I'm excited" in different emotional tones, happy, sarcastic or annoyed. This shows how tone changes the meaning of the words.

Emotion Role-Play: Create scenarios where the participants have to convey specific emotions through tone, for example delivering good news with enthusiasm or addressing a mistake with concern.

Volume and Projection

To communicate, one has to speak loud without having to raise the tone of his voice to the extent of causing Überoi's ears to ring. Techniques include:

Diaphragmatic Breathing: Instruct the participants on how to do diaphragmatic breathing for reinforcement of loud speaking. This is deep breathing that creates a large space from the diaphragm and ensures that you have a strong and well pitched voice.

Volume Control Exercises: Each student should take turns speaking softly and deeply, to shout and enunciate properly. This assists the participants to modulate the loudness of their voices depending on the kind of environment.

2. Body Language

Posture and Gestures

This paper tests the hypothesis that body language influences the reception of messages. Activities to improve posture and gestures:Activities to improve posture and gestures:

Mirror Exercises: Bring the participants opposite to each other and make them sit/stand in an equal manner as their partner. It helps in creating awareness of other strategies of communication and assists in eradicating poor communication behaviours.

Posture Awareness: Teach about the aspects of body language and teaching how to adopt proper open and confident stances. They can for instance, perform standing tall, with back straight as a way of expressing confidence.

Facial Expressions

Facial expressions convey emotion and intention. Exercises to improve facial expressiveness:

Emotion Games: Play a game where the participants have to guess the emotion based on facial expressions only. This sharpens their ability to read and express emotion nonverbally.

Mirror Practice: Have the participants practise different facial expressions in front of a mirror to become more aware of their facial movements.

Eye Contact

Eye contact is key to effective communication. Exercises include:

Eye Contact Practice: Pair the participants to maintain eye contact while talking, gradually increasing the time. This builds comfort and engagement.

Eye Contact in Presentation: Practise making eye contact with different parts of the audience during presentations to connect with the listeners.

3. Active Listening

Reflective Listening

Reflective listening means understanding and showing empathy. Techniques include:

Role-Play Scenarios: Use role-play scenarios where one person explains a problem and the other reflects back what they heard.

Feedback Sessions: Have people give feedback on each other's reflective listening skills, on accuracy and empathy.

Empathy

Caring or understanding the other person is crucial in matters of interaction or relation. Exercises include:

Empathy Scenarios: Perform tasks that should teach how to appreciate and assure people. Examples for the practical application when people are forced to respond with understanding to a colleague.

Perspective-Taking: Ask participants to look at situations from another person's point of view and ask them the feelings and treatment the intended person might require.

Improving Corporate Communication

Using theatre techniques in corporate communication can be applied in many situations - presentations, meetings, one to one.

1. Presentations

Storytelling Structure

Most presentations follow a storytelling structure with a beginning, middle and end. Workshops can teach:

Narrative Construction: Learn to structure presentations as stories, using a narrative arc to hook the audience. Analyse successful presentations to see what works.

Personal Stories: Encourage the use of personal stories to make presentations more relevant and engaging.

Opening and Closing

Grabbing the audience's attention at the start and leaving a lasting impression at the end is key:The focus must be made to capture the viewers from the beginning and to make a good lasting impression at the end.

Attention-Grabbing Techniques: This is among the strategies other than statistics, questions, or quotes when starting a speech.

Memorable Closings: Reinforce the ability to write and give the concluding part that usually reiterates the main intention and the navigating direction.

2. Meetings

Agenda Setting

Meetings start with a clear agenda. Training can include:

Agenda Design: Learn to design agendas that prioritise the key issues and allocate time accordingly. This keeps meetings on track and efficient.

Objective Setting: Teach participants to set objectives for each agenda item so the meeting has purpose and outcome.

Facilitation Skills

Facilitation ensures inclusive and productive meetings:

Discussion Management: Use role-plays to practise managing discussions so everyone gets a chance to contribute. This develops skills in leading conversations and keeping them on track.

Conflict Mediation: Teach techniques for mediating conflicts and reaching consensus in meetings.

3. Interpersonal Communication

One to One

One to one communication is key to building relationships and resolving issues:

Role-Play Exercises: Practise one to one conversations focusing on active listening, empathy and clear expression of thoughts. This develops participants' ability to communicate in personal interactions.

Feedback Techniques: Teach how to give and receive feedback constructively.

Conflict Resolution

Resolving conflicts: Introducing them there and resolving conflicts constructively is very important for the healthy work environment.

Conflict Scenarios: Real life conflicts may be portrayed through role participants and this should be done in role plays. Teach skills on how to solve conflict with an aim of getting to understand each other, bargaining and concessions.

Mediation Skills: Gain competencies in conflict resolution of one employee with another towards promoting sanity and decency in the workplace.

Workshops and Exercises

Interactive workshops and exercises to practise and sharpen your communication skills using theatre techniques.

1. Voice Exercises

Reading Aloud

Reading with different emotions and pitches modulates:

Emotion and Pitch Variation: Read with different emotions and pitches to become more expressive and engaging.

Poetry Reading: Use poetry to play with tone and rhythm.

Vocal Warm-Ups

Vocal warm-ups get you speaking ready:

Humming and Lip Trills: Do humming, lip trills and scales to warm up the voice. These exercises relax the vocal cords and clarify.

Breath Control: Practise deep breathing to support projection and control.

2. Body Language Drills

Mirror Exercises

Mirror exercises develop body awareness:

Movement Mimicking: Pair participants and have them mirror each other's movements to become more aware of their body language.

Gesture Analysis: Analyse and discuss different gestures and how they impact communication.

Role-Playing

Role-playing scenarios develop body language:

Presentation Practice: Use role-playing to practise body language in different scenarios, such as presenting or having a difficult conversation. Focus on open and confident posture, right gestures and facial expressions.

Scenario Variation: Vary the scenarios to include different contexts, such as networking events, team meetings or client interactions to develop versatile body language.

3. Listening Circles

Group Discussions

Listening circles encourage active listening and feedback:
Discussion Rounds: Have participants share their thoughts while others listen actively. Feedback on communication style and listening.
Reflection Sessions: Reflect on what was heard, discuss key points and emotions to deepen understanding and empathy.

Listening Exercises

Exercises on listening skills improve comprehension and empathy:
Story Listening: Use exercises where participants listen to a short story and then discuss what they heard, focusing on details and emotions. This helps them listen more intently and accurately.
Empathy Mapping: The misconception is in enlarging the circles of empathy based on the auditor's level of listening, feelings, and perceptions to enhance the consideration of things heard.

Conclusion

The 'soft skills' especially the communication skills are important in the business world today. By using core theatre techniques like voice modulation, body language and active listening individuals can connect with others and get their message across. Practical workshops and exercises allow you to practise and sharpen these skills so they become part of your daily communication. As we continue to explore theatre and business we will find more ways to grow personally and organisationally.

V

Leadership and Team Building

Theatre as a Leadership Tool

Theatre techniques are a powerful way to develop leadership skills. By being a director, leaders can learn to articulate a vision, adapt to change and inspire their teams.

1. Leading Like a Director

Vision and Communication

A leader's ability to communicate a clear vision is key to leading a team:Of all the leadership qualities, it is in one's capacity to relay the leader's vision that makes a team:

Visionary Speeches: It can be dedicated to the training sessions that are aimed at creation and performing of the visionary speech. As leaders, they often rehearse how they would design their vision so that it sounds inspiring when they speak about it to the staff and it is done using narratives and proper tonality.

Storytelling Workshops: Organise sessions in which leaders tell stories as a means of practically exploring the topic. This entails outlining the kind of message that the organisation wants to pass in a story form that has a sequence of events and / or a call for an appeal to emotions.

Adaptability

Adaptability is key to good leadership, being able to respond to unexpected change and challenges:

Improvisation Games: Use improvisation games to develop quick thinking and adaptability. Scenarios can include sudden changes in business plans or unexpected team dynamics, requiring leaders to think on their feet and make quick decisions.

Scenario-Based Training: Create scenarios that mirror real life challenges, such as a crisis or significant change. Leaders practise their strategies and communication styles for the situation.

2. Motivating and Inspiring Teams

Positive Reinforcement

Giving positive feedback and reinforcement helps to motivate and inspire teams:

Constructive Feedback Role-Play: Role-play scenarios where leaders practise giving constructive feedback. This includes balancing positive reinforcement with constructive criticism to improve and maintain morale.

Recognition Programs: Develop programs that recognise and reward team achievements. Leaders can practise delivering recognition speeches that highlight individual and team contributions.

Collaborative Problem-Solving

Collaboration is the key to solving complex problems and innovation:

Group Exercises: Run workshops on collaborative problem-solving techniques. Use group exercises to tackle hypothetical scenarios, get teams to brainstorm, discuss and develop solutions together.

Facilitated Discussions: Facilitate discussions where teams look at real life problems and work together to find solutions. This develops a collaborative mindset and team dynamics.

Ensemble Building

Building an ensemble is key to achieving the goal. Trust exercises and activities that promote collaboration will strengthen the team.

1. Trust Exercises

Trust Falls

Trust falls are old school exercises that build trust in the team:

Trust Fall Variations: Try different variations of trust falls (side falls or forward falls) to increase the challenge and deepen the trust.

Debrief Sessions: After each exercise have participants talk about how they felt and what happened, to reinforce the importance of trust in the team.

Blindfolded Walks

Blindfolded walks build trust and communication:

Guided Walks: Pair participants up, with one blindfolded and the other guiding. This builds trust and sharpens communication skills as the guide has to clearly and accurately direct their partner.

Obstacle Courses: Create obstacle courses for blindfolded walks to add complexity and encourage problem solving and collaboration.

2. Creating a Collaborative Culture

Team-Building Activities

Activities that require teamwork and resourcefulness create a collaborative culture:Activities that require teamwork and resourcefulness create a collaborative culture:

Resource-Limited Challenges: This includes things such as task orientated activities like building a tower with limited materials. This helps to engage the participants whereby they are forced to consult, contribute and develop each member of the team's potential.

Escape Room Challenges: Hire a company that specialises in designing escape rooms and recreate the cases when the employees are to solve the task and complete the activities within the time limit to encourage teamwork and communication.

Open Forums

Regular open forums for team members to share ideas and feedback:

Idea-Sharing Sessions: Have regular sessions where team members can present ideas and provide feedback. This opens up communication and makes everyone feel heard and valued.

Anonymous Feedback Tools: Use anonymous feedback tools to get honest feedback from team members, to address any issues and improve the collaborative culture.

Activities for Corporate Teams

Theatre activities can be adapted for corporate teams to boost creativity, communication and leadership skills.

2. Theatre Games

"Yes, And" Game

The "Yes, And" game promotes acceptance and creativity:

Game Rules: Participants build on each other's ideas by saying "Yes, and...". This game gets participants to listen and contribute positively, to a collaborative mindset.

Application to Brainstorming: Apply the principles of the game to brainstorming sessions where all ideas are accepted and built upon, to increase creativity and innovation.

Status Games

Status games look at power dynamics and communication styles within the team:

Role Reversal: Participants take on different status roles (high, medium, low) in different scenarios (meetings or negotiations). This helps them see how status affects communication and interaction.

Reflection and Discussion: After the games have been done, have a discussion on the impact of status on team dynamics and how to use that awareness to improve communication and collaboration.

2. Role-Based Exercises

Leadership Scenarios

Role-based exercises allow you to practise leadership in a controlled environment:

Leadership Challenges: Create scenarios where you take on leadership roles and lead the team through challenges, e.g. launching a new project or resolving a conflict. This develops decision making and leadership skills.

Feedback Loops: Give feedback during and after the exercises, on what's going well and what to improve.

Perspective Switching

Perspective-switching exercises help you see other roles in the team:

Role-Playing: Have people switch roles, e.g. a manager becomes an employee or vice versa. This builds empathy and understanding of other perspectives.

Team Discussions: Discuss the insights from switching roles and how this can improve team dynamics and collaboration.

Conclusion

Theatre techniques are useful tools for developing leadership and team building in a corporate environment. By applying the principles of vision, communication, adaptability and collaboration, leaders can inspire and motivate their teams to achieve the same goal. Through trust exercises, theatre games and role-based activities teams can build stronger bonds, improve communication and create a collaborative environment. As businesses continue to explore the intersection of theatre and leadership they will find new ways to achieve personal and organisational success.

VI
Creativity and Innovation

In the current business environment, flexibility and invention provision are crucial elements. This chapter focuses on how to foster creativity and a detailed step by step guide on how to use acting in the office and selected dramatic techniques to enhance creativity.

Creating a Creative Space

This is why in this case culture has to promote creativity since this is the foundation of innovation. This involves appreciating the prevalence of creativity in organisations and techniques of tackling it.

1. Creativity in Business

Case Studies

Apple: Apple catches success by its creativity and innovation. The firm also fosters innovation and this has led to the current products such as iPhone and MacBook with creative solutions to problems.

Netflix: Netflix also exemplifies how creative thinking reconfigures the firm's business model and content delivery system. With DVD rental to streaming to producing its own content, Netflix's innovation strategy is still making it the Masters of icon entertainment.

2. Theatre Exercises

Theatre exercises can help employees think creatively and approach problems with a new perspective.

Brainstorming Sessions

Good brainstorming sessions allow for free flowing ideas without immediate criticism.

Mind Mapping: Use mind mapping to visually map out ideas and see the connections between them. This helps participants see the bigger picture and come up with new ideas.

Rapid Ideation: Conduct brain writes where each participant is expected to generate as many ideas as they can in the given time. This fosters creativity and rubs out prejudice and inhibitions which are key elements of creativity.

Creative Problem Solving Workshops

Theatre exercises can be used to tackle business challenges creatively.

Role-Playing Scenarios: One can incorporate role-play to depict typical business scenarios and encourage the participants to look at it and suggest solutions. For example they might specifically dress up as different stakeholders in order to have different viewpoints.

Storytelling Exercises: Get participants to tell stories around a business challenge. This gets them to think about different approaches and outcomes.

Improvisation Techniques

Innovating techniques like that are perfect for if you need to think on your feet. Introduce some of the principles of comedy to help develop a better environment of creativity while brainstorming in order to arrive at better ideas.

1. Basics of Improvisation

Know the rules of improv to tap into its creative power.

Improv Rules

Accepting Offers: Teach people to accept and add to each other's ideas instead of rejecting them. This creates a positive atmosphere.

Building on Ideas: Teach people to add to ideas instead of critiquing them immediately. This keeps the creativity flowing and encourages more thinking outside the box.

Short Form Games

Short form improv games are great for quick thinking and spontaneity.

Word Association: In this game, people say a word related to the previous word. This exercise helps them make connections and think on their feet.

Scenes from a Hat: People draw random scene suggestions from a hat and improvise short scenes. This game encourages creativity and flexibility.

2. Improv in Brainstorming Sessions

Improving brainstorming sessions will help creativity and collaboration.

Yes, And

Building on Ideas: Use the "Yes, And" technique to add to ideas without criticism. People accept each idea and add to it, creating a chain of ideas.

Collaborative Environment: This creates a collaborative environment where all ideas are valued and you get more diverse and creative solutions.

Improv Storytelling

Group Storytelling: Have people do group storytelling exercises where they add one sentence at a time to a story. This encourages collaboration and helps them think as a team.

Creative Flow: These exercises help people get into a creative flow and generate and refine ideas.

Case Studies

Looking at how other companies use creativity and theatre techniques can be useful and inspiring.

1. Google

Google Company is well-known for its creative culture and work environment all over the world.

Innovation Labs

Improv Techniques: Google adopts the methods of drama to foster imagination and new ideas. For instance in the innovation labs games such as improve are used in order to generate and further ideas.

Collaborative Spaces: There is also the comfort, more thinking outside the box and collaboration, typical working spaces in Google for instance are open and blended with colours and have discussion areas.

Workshops

Creative Workshops: Google has drama sessions in which its workers play drama to enhance their creativity. These workshops consist of, but not limited to, Improv Playing, Role Playing, and Narration Playing.

2. IDEO

The design and innovation based consultancy, IDEO, incorporates theatre into their methods of design thinking.

Design Thinking

Theatre Integration: Role playing and improvisation acts as a means for IDEO to discover new ideas when simulating the users. These techniques are useful for entering the user's perspective and to produce ideas within designers.

Empathy Exercises: It means that during the use of such activity as role-playing and other theatre exercises the IDEO designers can be initiated to the world and experiences of their users.

Creative Workshops

Innovation Workshops: Ways of teachings: IDEO holds many sessions portraying acting styles as a way of inspiring creation.

Such workshops use acting in particular, and dramatisation in general, in combination with brainstorming and storytelling to assist people in finding solutions to multifaceted issues.

Co-Creation: Finally, IDEO deems the concept of co-creation, making teams make theatre to get ideas that are then developed actively.

Conclusion

Creativity and innovation are key to business success and theatre techniques are a powerful tool to create a creative environment. By running brainstorming sessions, creative problem solving workshops and improvisation exercises businesses can generate more ideas and solutions. Case studies from Google and IDEO show how these approaches can drive creativity and innovation. As businesses continue to explore the intersection of theatre and business creativity they will find new ways to stay ahead of the game.

VII
Stress Management and Wellbeing

Stress management and wellbeing are key to a healthy workplace. Theatre offers tools for emotional expression, mindfulness and practical stress relief. This chapter looks at how theatre can be used in the corporate world.

Theatre and Wellbeing

Theatre is a way to explore and manage emotions, be mindful and build a supportive community.

1. Emotional Expression and Release

Emotions help one cope with stress and are a noble component of human wellbeing. Role play is acceptable as a form of behaviour rehearsal because through theatre, an individual gets to understand methods of discharging the emotional build-up in himself or herself in a safe manner.

Role-Playing for Emotional Exploration

Exercise: The situations that are exhibited to participants may lead to stress, joy, sadness or anger among them. The performers actually carry out such roles in twos or threes for the purpose of displaying and venting feelings.

Example Scenario: An intense quarrel with a colleague or a warm family dinner with familiar people.

Benefit: It assists participants get rid of stress and builds up empathy since whoever is being mimicked practically feels the role they are mimicking for some time.

Monologue Exercises

Exercise: Participants write and perform monologues based on their own experiences, to express themselves fully.

Benefit: This activity releases emotions and provides a space to share personal stories, builds community and support.

2. Mindfulness and Presence

Mindfulness practices reduce stress by being present in the moment. Theatre techniques can increase mindfulness and presence.

Presence Exercises

Exercise: Orientation that involves having the participants close their eyes for a moment and take turns to describe what they see, hear, smell, taste and feel; this helps to bring them back to the room and the present time.

Benefit: Stimulates awareness, leads to the decrease in anxiety because the focus is in the present time.

Mindful Movement

Exercise: Slow, deliberate movement, e.g. walking across the room with full attention to each step or a simple dance with full attention to each movement.

Benefit: Increases mindfulness and body awareness.

Practical Techniques

Adding practical theatre-based techniques to stress management programs can be very effective and beneficial overall.

1. Drama Therapy Basics

Drama therapy, therefore, involves the application of theatrical techniques with a view of handling psychological and emotional problems.

Role-Play

Exercise: The following are some of the conditions that may lead to stress at the workplaces ; Arrangement of the following scenario should be made and subjects should be encouraged to demonstrate how they can handle stressed factors –conflict with the boss, working under pressure to meet the deadline.

Benefit: It guarantees that most of the various approaches that are employed in the handling of stress can be tried out in the participants within the experiment.

Group Storytelling

Exercise: Participants create and tell a story together, each adding a part that reflects their own experiences or feelings.

Benefit: Encourages group sharing and connection.

2. Relaxation Exercises

Sometimes the originating stress lies at the workplace which if not controlled may lead to physical and mental illnesses; the following relaxation exercises help in the reduction of stress.

Guided Imagery

Exercise: Sometimes, lead the participants to visualise a calm place or the positive result, and let them try to think of each of the senses.

Benefit: Helps in eliminating stress and anxiety as it provides the mind with something else to focus on, thus offering the mind a chance to calm down.

Deep Breathing

Exercise: Instruct the participants on 4-7-8 breathing exercises and apply it in the sessions.

Benefit: Decrease of the manifestation of physical stress.

Workshops and Activities

Having regular workshops and activities around stress management and wellbeing can create a more supportive workplace.

1. Emotional Check-Ins

Starting meetings with emotional check-ins creates a supportive space and increases emotional awareness.

Start of Meetings

Exercise: Start meetings with a quick round where participants share a word or phrase that describes how they are feeling.

Benefit: Creates a supportive space.

Emotion Wheels

Exercise: Use emotion wheels to help participants identify and express their feelings during check-ins.

Benefit: Provides a visual tool to help participants understand and articulate their emotions.

2. Mindfulness Sessions

Having regular mindfulness sessions can help employees develop habits that reduce stress over time.

Regular Sessions

Exercise: In SD1, arrange to practise mindfulness with different techniques of breathing techniques/ exercising, guided meditation, and walking meditation, on a weekly basis.

Benefit: Repetition strengthens the muscles of concentration and worry regulation; it strengthens the foundation of mindfulness.

Mindfulness Retreats

Exercise: Run half-day or full-day mindfulness retreats where employees can fully immerse themselves in mindfulness practices.

Benefit: More intense experience, deeper relaxation and stress relief.

3. Theatre Games for Stress Relief

Theatre games can be a fun way to relieve stress and build a team.

Freeze Game

Exercise: Participants act out a scene and freeze on command. Others take over and change the scene, encouraging creativity and stress relief.

Benefit: Quick thinking and adaptability, fun way to release stress.

Emotion Circle

Exercise: Participants stand in a circle and take turns expressing emotions, releasing tension and increasing emotional awareness.

Benefit: Emotional intelligence, safe space to express.

Conclusion

Theatre techniques are powerful tools for stress management and wellbeing in the workplace. By combining emotional expression, mindfulness and practical stress release strategies businesses can create a supportive and healthy environment. Regular workshops and activities around these techniques will help employees manage stress better and overall wellbeing and productivity will improve. As businesses explore the intersection of theatre and corporate wellbeing they will find new ways to support employees' mental and emotional health.

VIII
Diversity and Inclusion

Diversity and inclusion is very crucial in ensuring that the workforce continues to be healthy and raging. It is for this reason that theatre techniques can be employed with a view of developing means that will change the perception of employees and ensure that they become willing instruments in the development of social causes. This chapter looks at how theatre can be used in the corporate world.

Theatre for Social Awareness

Theatre can be a great way to address biases and social awareness.

1. Challenging Biases through Role-Play

Role play can highlight biases and discriminatory behaviour, so participants can experience and address these in a safe space.

Scenario-Based Role-Play

Exercise: Create role-play scenarios that highlight common biases and discriminatory behaviour. Participants take on different roles to experience and address these.

Example Scenario: A hiring process where implicit biases affect decision-making, or a team meeting where some voices are ignored.

Benefit: This exercise helps participants to recognise and address biases, to be more inclusive.

Forum Theatre

Exercise: Participants act out scenes of oppression or discrimination and then pause to discuss and explore different solutions. The audience can suggest changes and the actors replay the scene with those changes.

Benefit: Participants have to find solutions to real life problems, to get a deeper understanding of diversity issues.

2. Building Empathy and Understanding

Compassionate understanding of an employee generates equality in the workforce. Therefore, the theatre exercises can assist the participants in getting a better perception of other individuals.

Perspective-Taking Exercises

Exercise: Role play or simulation where people put on a maid, child or any other character to be able to get or feel the same situation. For example, assume to be a person with a different experience of the day.

Benefit: Relates the hero to the common man and makes him appear ordinary.

Empathy Mapping

Exercise: Participants create empathy maps to see and understand how others feel, think and experience.

Benefit: A tool to develop empathy and improve relationships.

Inclusive Workplaces

It becomes evident that through the use of theatre, diversity and, in turn, an environment of acceptance, can be achieved in the workplace.

1. Theatre Techniques to Explore Diversity

Doing theatrical exercises can lead to open conversations about diversity and inclusion.

Diversity Dialogues

Exercise: Have participants use theatre techniques to share their experiences and perspectives on diversity.

Benefit: Encourages open communication and deeper understanding of diversity.

Story Circles

Exercise: I have found different techniques such as people taking a seat in a circle and then everyone can tell a story they have encountered regarding diversity and inclusion. Always give everyone a turn and use cues to get people started and to make sure that they say something.

Benefit: Promotes unity in the group/organisation.

2. Culture of Inclusion

Incorporating inclusive practices and diversity committees can create a more supportive workplace.

Inclusive Practices

Exercise: Open forums, regular diversity training, inclusive decision making.
  Benefit: More inclusive workplace.

Diversity Committees

Exercise: Form a committee to promote diversity and inclusion, use theatre to facilitate and lead initiatives.
  Benefit: A structured approach to diversity and inclusion in the organisation.

Case Studies

Looking at real life examples can show how theatre can be used in diversity and inclusion initiatives.

1. PwC

Unconscious Bias Training

Detail: PwC uses theatre based training to address unconscious bias, role-playing and group discussion.
  Example Exercise: Role-playing different scenarios where unconscious bias might occur, followed by group discussion to reflect on the experience.

Inclusive Leadership Programs

Detail: PwC uses role-playing and storytelling in their leadership programs to promote inclusive behaviour.

Example Exercise: Leaders role-play scenarios where they have to navigate diversity challenges and reflect on their actions.

2. Microsoft

Empathy Workshops

Detail: Microsoft uses role-playing exercises to build empathy and understanding among staff.

Example Exercise: Participants enact a selected scenario where they get an opportunity to view life from a different viewpoint then engage in a group discussion as to what they have learned.

Diversity and Inclusion Initiatives

Detail: Microsoft uses theatre to increase inclusivity and diversity in the organisation.

Example Exercise: Forum Theatre where staff act out and discuss solutions to diversity challenges.

Conclusion

The incorporation of theatre in diversity and inclusion programs make the staff more understanding and aware. To reduce biases and increase understanding of other's views, businesses can: Role-play to eliminate prejudices, Perspective-taking to engage with empathy, and diversity dialogues/story circles to promote an open company. Many of the clients of Pricewaterhousecoopers (PWC) and Microsoft executives have adopted the above-mentioned strategies, and the following examples explain how this has taken place: Incorporating theatre in the future as businesses attempt to find new strategies to open employees' eyes and increase diversity; it would go a long way to making workspaces more diverse and inclusive.

IX
Practical Implementation

That is why, presenting and implementing the theatre based programme in the framework of a business organisation presupposes both reflecting, proclamation and constant assessment of determinative goals. The reader will learn in this chapter how to design and present a theatre based program that addresses your corporate audience.

Designing a Theatre Based Program

This paper therefore concludes that a theatre based programme development consists of defining objectives, designing its content as well as how the trainers are to be trained.

1. Objectives

To ensure the program is relevant to the needs of the organisation, one has to define objectives or goals and the target user group.

Clear Objectives

Exercise: What do you want to achieve with the theatre based program? Objectives could be improving communication skills, leadership, creativity or wellbeing.

Example: A goal might be to improve team working and reduce communication breakdowns.

Benefit: Clear objectives give direction and help measure the program's success.

Target Audience

Exercise: Who is the target audience for the program? What are their specific needs and challenges?

Example: The target audience might be middle managers who need to develop their leadership skills.

Benefit: By tailoring the program to the audience the content will be relevant and effective.

2. Structuring the Program

A good program balances theory, practical exercises and real life applications.

Balanced Content

Exercise: Develop a content that includes a mix of theory, practical exercises and real life applications. Make the program interactive and fun.

Example: A 6 week program that covers communication skills, leadership, creativity and stress management.

Benefit: A balanced content keeps participants engaged and develops all skills.

Session Design

Exercise: Design sessions that build on each other, starting with simple concepts and moving to complex techniques.

Example: Start with simple voice modulation exercises and move to complex role-playing scenarios.

Benefit: Progressive session design helps participants build confidence and master skills step by step.

3. Facilitator Training

Facilitators are key to the program's success. They need to be trained in theatre techniques and corporate training methods.

Skills Development

Exercise: Educate those who are facilitating the training in the theatrical skills and corporate training methodologies. Ensure that they are fine with acting, face and creating groups and exercises.

Example: Usually, a workshop for the facilitator during which he/she is introduced to basic principles of theatre and its implementation in the business environment.

Benefit: Trained facilitators can lead participants and the program will be successful.

Resources and Materials

Exercise: Give facilitators the resources they need, such as lesson plans, exercises and evaluation tools.

Example: A facilitator guide that includes instructions for each exercise.

Benefit: Access to resources means facilitators are well prepared and can deliver consistent and effective sessions.

Evaluation and Feedback

Ongoing evaluation and feedback is key to measuring the program and making changes.

1. Measuring the Impact

Use surveys and metrics to measure the program.

Surveys and Assessments

Exercise: Use pre and post program surveys to measure changes in skills, behaviours and attitudes.

Example: A survey that measures communication skills before and after the program.

Benefit: Surveys give you quantitative data to measure the program.

Performance Metrics

Exercise: Track metrics related to the program objectives such as communication effectiveness, leadership performance and creative output.

Example: Number of team projects completed after the program.

Benefit: Metrics give you objective measures of the program and areas to improve.

2. Continuous advancement

Collecting feedback and making changes means the program stays relevant and effective.

Feedback Collection

Exercise: Collect feedback from participants and facilitators to identify strengths and areas to improve.

Example: An anonymous feedback form after each session.

Benefit: Feedbacks help to identify whether something is good or bad or simply inform you of the condition that is in the market.

Program Adjustments

Exercise: Use the feedback to make changes to the program so it stays relevant and effective.

Example: Adding more practical exercises to the curriculum based on participant feedback.

Benefit: Continuous advancement keeps the program fresh and responsive to participant needs.

Conclusion

It can be concluded that theatre activity in the corporate environment needs organisation and blueprints developed in advanced, efficient implementation of the planned measures, and continuous assessment of the outcomes. Thus, by setting objectives and outcomes, designing a curriculum, developing and evaluating facilitators' skills, and assessing the effectiveness of the program, organisations can develop and enhance the usage of theatre in the areas of communication, leadership, imagination, and well-being of the working team. When theatre is introduced into organisational settings it is always a continuous advancement and flexibility that make organisational programs such as theatre yield long term benefits and a more engaged workforce.

X

The Role of the Corporate Theatre Trainer

The corporate theatre trainer is thus both a theatre practitioner as well as professional skill trainer and development expert with both the creative and the interpersonal skills harmony and combination of business skills and performing arts. The actual job entails far more than vast knowledge of theatrical practices or theatre pedagogy: this person has to be fully conscious of corporate processes and ways, as well as be capable to channel artistic principles into actual training strategies. This chapter will aim at identifying the duties that the corporate theatre trainer is supposed to perform, the kind of skills that one should possess, and some performing tips that could be applied to create effective training sessions.

Role Clarification of the Corporate Theatre Trainer

Bridging Two Worlds

Thus, the corporate theatre trainer works in between arts and business helping him corporations solving such problems as communication, leadership, team building and creativity using tools of theatre. This position requires the person to appreciate the peculiarity of the corporate clients and design the theatre based activities in relation with the needs of the clients.

Facilitating Transformation

Fundamentally, the corporate theatre trainer is involved in the process of change. Whether it is aimed at improving the communicative competencies of an employee, increasing the cohesion of a team, or facilitating innovation, the trainer's purpose is to bring change.

Key Responsibilities of the Corporate Theatre Trainer

Needs Assessment

The kinds of programs or initiatives that may benefit from corporate theatre training may not be apparent to a trainer at first instance, and this is why analysis must be conducted before any program is launched. Here one has to take into consideration the opportunities and threats inherent in a particular organisation and determine its needs and desires in the short and long term.

Example: Suppose, a trainer is assigned to a client, who is a tech company; she or he may realise that the main problem is a communication barrier within the organisation. This insight will be useful in informing the training program that needs to be developed for the employees.

Program Design and Development

After the needs assessment is done, the trainer comes up with a training programme to be implemented. This relates to identifying and implementing proper theatre techniques and exercise, which meet the objectives of the organisation.

Example: In reference to the above-described tech company, the trainer could incorporate the development of listening skills through games like improvisation and incorporate schemes of role-playing through different department heads to strengthen cooperation between the departments of the company.

Delivering Training Sessions

The best place that the skills of the corporate theatre trainer come out clearly is the delivery of training sessions. This is not only about conducting the exercises and engaging activities but also about setting the mood and the conditions that would make participants eager to try new behaviour and use new techniques.

Example: In the course of a simulation, perhaps while practising how to deliver an unpleasant message, the trainer can then demonstrate the process and make suggestions as to how the communication could be done better.

Providing Feedback and Coaching

It can be stated that feedback plays an important role in the process of training. Also, the corporate theatre trainer has to be proficient in delivering feedback that can be constructive in informing the participants of their strong suits and the aspects they still require improvement on.

Example: When one participant has done a performance, the trainer can approach him and say, 'You used good non-verbal cues there,' while at the same time pointing out to the participant whose voice was low that he or she needed to speak louder.

Evaluating Program Effectiveness

This is because the usual trainer in the corporate theatre training program is charged with the responsibility of conducting an assessment of the correspondence of the training program to its goal. This is done through procuring participants' and stakeholders' feedback; evaluating changes in patient behaviours and their overall performance; and where necessary, modification.

Example: The trainer may employ questionnaires before and after training to determine the extent of change in communication and can also have periodic sessions to enhance on learned behaviours.

Essential Skills and Attributes

Theatre Expertise

An element of degree of proficiency in the techniques used in theatres is compulsory. These are performance skills in areas like ad libbing, voice control, gesture control and narration.

Example: An expert in the use of improvisation can explain and facilitate participants boosting their time-sensitive decision-making skills which are very sparing in the contemporary business world.

Corporate Savvy

It is equally significant to understand the corporate environment, of which the firm is a part of. Organisations must also learn about the difficulties and realities within various sectors as well as the business climate so that proper training strategies can be established.

Example: A trainer employed in a financial services firm may set his objectives more on the accuracy of communication that is characteristic of the industry.

Empathy and Emotional Intelligence

Empathy helps to comprehend the participant's situation and ensure comfort during training. Emotional intelligence here assists the trainer to understand the group dynamics as well as being able to properly correct those who are in the wrong.

Example: The trainer might know that a participant is nervous about an acting exercise and might give support and encouragement to ensure they succeed.

Communication Skills

First, it is critical to consider communication as one of the key components of the trainer stakeholders' interaction, with the trainer being in the centre of the communication process. This can be regarding the explanation of exercises, remedy provision as well as debates.

Example: In a provided instance, the trainer may give clear and clear instructions when facilitating a complicated role play activity in order that all stakeholders understand what's expected of them.

Flexibility and Adaptability

Training sessions within the corporation might be unanticipated and the trainer has to be capable of responding to hidden circumstances and participants themselves.

Example: If a planned exercise is creating a lot of rebellion, the trainer might soon divert to another exercise that will capture the essence of the participants.

Effective strategies for training process

Creating a Healthy and Safe Environment

Creation of a safe environment is critical for training to take place. These include trust; social interaction or free flowing communication and participant solidarity.

Example: The trainer may have demographic or interpersonal icebreakers at the beginning of each session to ensure that people can associate well.

Employing a Multitude of Approaches

It makes the training sessions more interesting when different techniques from theatre arts are incorporated in training; this also takes into consideration learners' multiple intelligences.

Example: A session could consist of a combination of, say, three activities out of improvisation, role-play, and storytelling, in such a way that all the people present get an experience of all the activities.

Encouraging Active Participation

Another finding of the study was that it is essential to enrol and engage the subjects in theatre-based training fully. It is the trainer's responsibility to ensure that everyone can participate and is willing to step out of his/her comfort zone.

Example: The trainer might employ the "Yes, and" exercise to ensure that the trainees support each other's suggestions so that the environment is positive.

Ensuring instructions and feedback is clear

There is a necessity to give clear instructions and also provide the participants with specific feedback to understand what they do wrong and how they can correct it.

Example: he/she might then, depending on the training exercise used, perhaps a role-playing exercise, give them specific feedback of what the participant has done right and possible suggestions on how to do it better.

Customising programs to participant needs

participant's life should also be taken into consideration when developing or modifying programs for a certain group of learners.

In other words, every single training must be designed taking in consideration the learning and development requirements of the participants. This entails one to willingly change and incorporate the feedback.

Example: If the participants are finding it difficult to execute any of the exercises that have been set, then the trainer might continue to add more time to help the participants understand the area better.

Conclusion

The corporate theatre trainer has a very crucial job that is at the same time quite rewarding. These trainers have the possibility to change the organisations for the better, enhance the required skills of the people and make the workplace more creative and productive through theatre.

When you start your career as a theatre trainer, do not consider solely your assignments as presenting; it's your job to give audiences memorable experiences and designed training activities that lead to personal and work accomplishment. Always observe the theatrical tenets, be aware of your subjects' requirements and bend on improvising. The change that can be created is significant and the scope is only as limited as one's imagination.

The Future of Theatre in Corporate

Thus, theatre in the workplace has demonstrated a good outcome. Here are some trends and developments that will further strengthen the position of theatre in training and development in the future.

1. Trends and Predictions

Virtual Theatre Workshops

Detail: Given the modern trends in the world and the growing availability of distance work and digital transformations, virtual classes in theatre are possible. These workshops help to deliver theatre to the remote teams and no office is too far away.

Example: An online business simulation in which people from various places collaborate in a synchronous environment to solve a business-related case. The participants can also be doing some exercise and even receive real time feedback and interact as if everybody is in one room through the video conferencing tools.

Benefit: Theatrical performance workshops enhance co-teamwork and relations, public speaking, and innovation ability all in one single training while taking into consideration the emergent model of working that has workers spread across different regions.

Digital Storytelling

Detail: Digital storytelling is gradually finding its way into the corporate training arena and as a method of sending messages and even motivating the employees. Digital media tools can be integrated with other methods of training familiar to the companies thus making it possible to design more engrossing and relevant materials.

Example: Creating and sharing stories on digital platforms that illustrate key training concepts. For example an animated video that follows a character through various workplace scenarios, showing effective communication and leadership skills.

Benefit: Digital storytelling makes training more engaging and memorable so employees can better understand and retain information.

Immersive Theatre Experiences

Detail: Immersive theatre experiences where participants are part of the narrative offer new ways to train and develop employees. These experiences can simulate real life business scenarios, where participants can practise skills in a controlled but dynamic environment.

Example: An immersive training session where participants navigate a simulated business crisis. They might have to make decisions, communicate with stakeholders and manage team dynamics under pressure.

Benefit: Immersive theatre experiences provide hands-on learning opportunities to develop critical thinking, problem solving and leadership skills.

2. Ongoing Research and Developments

Research Initiatives

Detail: Ongoing research into the benefits and applications of theatre in corporate is key to moving the field forward. Various institutions and organisations are leading the way in exploring how theatre can improve employee performance, engagement and overall workplace culture.

Example: Research into the impact of theatre training on employee performance and engagement. These studies can provide evidence of what works and what doesn't.

Benefit: Research helps to prove the benefits of theatre training, inform best practice and future development.

New Practices

Detail: Similarly, as the technological field develops the new practices that integrate theatre into corporate training also tend to evolve. Mobile applications and the use of new technologies also brought theatre to new levels such as augmented reality (AR) and virtual reality (VR).

Example: Extending the experience of serious applications of theatre training with augmented reality and virtual reality. Everyone dons VR headsets and performs in a 'virtual reality' environment in which such activities as negotiation, leadership style encounters or pressure tests are conducted.

Benefit: AR and VR, in a way that other teaching methods cannot, gives the students first hand experience.

Theatre in the workplace is not a trend, it's a transformation that can lead to more engaged, creative and inclusive workplaces. By applying the principles of theatre businesses can unlock new possibilities for growth and success and a more agile and responsive corporate culture. As we go forward the more we explore and innovate in this area the more valuable theatre will be for corporate development and training.

The work of bringing theatre into the workplace is never done, there's always more to create more effective, more engaging and more impactful training. By keeping up with the latest developments organisations can stay ahead of the curve and their workforce.

APPENDICES

Appendix A: Role-Playing Scenarios

Scenario 1: Tough Client

Objective: Conflict resolution and customer service

Background: Client is unhappy with product and wants a refund

Roles: Client, Customer Service Rep, Supervisor

Instructions: Act out the scenario with the client being upset and the rep trying to resolve the issue. Supervisor can step in if needed to help out.

Scenario 2: Team Challenge

Background: Project team has a tight deadline and needs to work together to get their tasks done.

Roles: Project Manager, Team Members

Instructions: Role-play a team meeting where team members discuss their tasks, identify the bottlenecks and come up with a plan to meet the deadline.

Appendix B: Voice Modulation Exercises

Exercise 1: Pitch Control

Activity: Read a passage flat, then re-read it with varying pitch to highlight.

Purpose: How does pitch help to emphasise the message?

Exercise 2: Emotion through Tone

Activity: Say the phrase "I'm excited" in different tones (happy, sarcastic, annoyed).
Purpose: Practise different emotions.

Appendix C: Improvisation Games

Game 1: Word Association

Instructions: The learners face each other in a circle. The tone is repeated and one member of the circle says a word, the following member utters the first word that he/ she can think of then it goes round a circle.
Purpose: Fast and prompt thinking together with innovation.

Game 2: Scenes from a Hat

Instructions: Prepare different scene prompts on the paper and fold them, putting them into a hat. Acting scene where participants have to act to a card that is pulled out of a hat.
Purpose: Improvisation and spontaneity.

Appendix D: Mindfulness Exercises

Exercise 1: Five Senses

Activity: They in turn use any one of the five senses to describe what they experience with ideas extended and elaborated by other members.

Purpose: Inform the audience and lower their stress levels.

Exercise 2: Mindful Movement

Activity: Slowly move across the room with full awareness of each step.

Purpose: Mindfulness and body awareness.

Appendix E: Evaluation Tools

Pre-Program Survey

Objective: What are participants skills, behaviours and attitudes before the program?

Pre-Program Survey

Sample Questions:

How comfortable are you with public speaking?

Rate your team collaboration skills.

How often do you think creatively at work?

Post-Program Survey

Sample Questions:

How has your comfort level with public speaking changed?

What have you improved in your team collaboration?

Give me examples of how you've applied creativity at work.

Appendix F: More to Read

Books:

"The Leader's Guide to Storytelling" by Stephen Denning
   "Impro: Improvisation and the Theatre" by Keith Johnstone
   "Daring Greatly" by Brené Brown

Articles:

"The Neuroscience of Leadership" by David Rock and Jeffrey Schwartz
   "Why Diversity Matters" by McKinsey & Company
   "The Benefits of Mindfulness in the Workplace" by Harvard Business Review

Websites:

TED Talks
   Theatre Communications Group
   Mindful

Appendix G: Templates and Worksheets

Template 1: Role-Play Scenario Planner

Objective:
   Background:
   Roles:
   Instructions:

Worksheet 1: Empathy Mapping

Section 1: What they see

Section 2: What they hear
Section 3: What they think and feel
Section 4: What they say and do

Worksheet 2: Story Circle Prompts

Share an experience where you would have felt valued at your workplace.

Even organisational leaders have once faced a challenge and this is an opportunity to share one of them.

Bibliography

Books

Boal, Augusto. Theatre of the Oppressed. Pluto Press, 2008.

Brown, Brené. Daring Greatly: How the Courage to Be Vulnerable Transforms the Way We Live, Love, Parent, and Lead. Avery, 2012.

Denning, Stephen. The Leader's Guide to Storytelling: Mastering the Art and Discipline of Business Narrative. Jossey-Bass, 2011.

Johnstone, Keith. Impro: Improvisation and the Theatre. Routledge, 1979.

Lipman, Doug. Improving Your Storytelling: Beyond the Basics for All Who Tell Stories in Work or Play. August House, 1999.

McKee, Robert. Story: Substance, Structure, Style, and the Principles of Screenwriting. ReganBooks, 1997.

Noland, Carrie. Agency and Embodiment: Performing Gestures/Producing Culture. Harvard University Press, 2009.

Rock, David, and Jeffrey Schwartz. Your Brain at Work: Strategies for Overcoming Distraction, Regaining Focus, and Working Smarter All Day Long. HarperBusiness, 2009.

Sinek, Simon. Start with Why: How Great Leaders Inspire Everyone to Take Action. Portfolio, 2009.

Stanislavski, Konstantin. An Actor Prepares. Theatre Arts Books, 1989.

Sternberg, Robert J. Handbook of Creativity. Cambridge University Press, 1998.

Bandura, Albert. Social Learning Theory. Prentice-Hall, 1977.

Burns, James MacGregor. Leadership. Harper & Row, 1978.

Csikszentmihalyi, Mihaly. Flow: The Psychology of Optimal Experience. Harper & Row, 1990.

Kolb, David A. Experiential Learning: Experience as the Source of Learning and Development. Prentice-Hall, 1984.

Seligman, Martin E.P., and Mihaly Csikszentmihalyi. Positive Psychology: An Introduction. American Psychological Association, 2000.

Sweller, John. Cognitive Load Theory. Psychology Press, 2011.

Gardner, Howard. Frames of Mind: The Theory of Multiple Intelligences. Basic Books, 1983.

Articles

Amabile, Teresa M. "How to Kill Creativity." Harvard Business Review, September-October 1998.

Brown, Brené. "The Power of Vulnerability." TED Talk. 2010.

Eagly, Alice H., and Linda L. Carli. "The Female Leadership Advantage: An Evaluation of the Evidence." The Leadership Quarterly, vol. 14, no. 6, 2003.

Rock, David, and Jeffrey Schwartz. "The Neuroscience of Leadership." Strategy+Business, May 30, 2006.

"Why Diversity Matters." McKinsey & Company, January 2015.

"The Benefits of Mindfulness in the Workplace." Harvard Business Review, January 2015.

Fredrickson, Barbara L. "The Broaden-and-Build Theory of Positive Emotions." Philosophical Transactions of the Royal Society B: Biological Sciences, 2004.

Goleman, Daniel. "What Makes a Leader?" Harvard Business Review, 1998.

Websites

TED Talks. https://www.ted.com/

Theatre Communications Group. https://www.tcg.org/

Mindful. https://www.mindful.org/

Harvard Business Review. https://hbr.org/
McKinsey & Company. https://www.mckinsey.com/
Strategy+Business. https://www.strategy-business.com/

Reports

"Global Human Capital Trends 2021." Deloitte Insights, 2021.
"The Future of Jobs Report 2020." World Economic Forum, October 2020.

Research Studies

Amabile, Teresa M., et al. "Creativity and the Role of the Leader." Harvard Business Review, October 2004.
Fredrickson, Barbara L., and Marcial F. Losada. "Positive Affect and the Complex Dynamics of Human Flourishing." American Psychologist, 2005.
Goleman, Daniel. "What Makes a Leader?" Harvard Business Review, November-December 1998.

Manuals and Guides

Lipman, Doug. Improving Your Storytelling: Beyond the Basics for All Who Tell Stories in Work or Play. August House, 1999.
McKee, Robert. Story: Substance, Structure, Style, and the Principles of Screenwriting. ReganBooks, 1997.

INDEX

www.ingramcontent.com/pod-product-compliance
Lightning Source LLC
Chambersburg PA
CBHW031434130726
47989CB00003B/1135